The Birth to My Purpose

The Journey to Motherhood

Motivator
Mikkita L Moore

The Birth to My Purpose
The Journey to Motherhood

The Birth to My Purpose
The Journey to Motherhood

Copyright © 2020 Mikkita L Moore and Invisible Daughter LLC. All Rights Reserved. No part of this book may be reproduced or transmitted in any form or by any means, electronic or mechanical, including photocopying, recording, or by any information storage or retrieval system except by a reviewer who may quote brief pages in a review to be printed in a magazine or newspaper, without written permission from the author. Unless otherwise stated, all Bible verses were taken from various versions of the Holy Bible.

ISBN: 978-1-7354792-3-1
Imprint: Invisible Daughter, LLC
Printed and bounded in the United States of America.

The Birth to My Purpose
The Journey to Motherhood

The Birth to My Purpose
The Journey to Motherhood

Thank You!!

The Birth to My Purpose
The Journey to Motherhood

The Birth to My Purpose
The Journey to Motherhood

Special Thanks & Dedication

Thank all of you for making this book possible

All the Authors: Mikkita L Moore, Latonya Willett, Alexis Chavers, Yolanda Givens, Paula Kendrick, and Dr. Stacy L Henderson!!

Graphic Designer: Shawn Robinson, of 727 Marketing... It's been a pleasure to work with you!!

This book is dedicated to all the ladies that is or has taken that amazing Journey to Womanhood... This one is for you!

The Birth to My Purpose
The Journey to Motherhood

The Birth to My Purpose
The Journey to Motherhood

Table of Contents

Chapter One: It Was Never A Mistake, **Mikkita L. Moore**

Chapter Two: A Parent That Didn't Really Know How to Parent, **Paula Kendrick**

Chapter Three: Steels Toes and Stilettos': Reflections of a Military Mom, **Dr. Stacy L Henderson**

Chapter Four: Sometimes You Have to Fight, **Latonya Willett**

Chapter Five: Unplanned… But Purpose Was Birthed, **Yolanda Givens**

Chapter Six: Purpose Birthed Through Pain, **Alexis Chavers**

The Birth to My Purpose
The Journey to Motherhood

The Birth to My Purpose
The Journey to Motherhood

Chapter One

It Was Never A Mistake

Mikkita L Moore

The Birth to My Purpose
The Journey to Motherhood

Mikkita L Moore, an author, motivational speaker and mother of five, starting at the tender age of 14 from the South Side of Chicago. Mikkita is a retired, master stylist and cosmetology instructor. She has owned two successful hair salons over a period of 13 years and an event-planning company, *Symply Plyzurez Eventz* since 2004. Mikkita is the CEO of Invisible Daughter LLC, which is the publishing company that specializes in Transparency writing, "Getting the Story Out". Mikkita is also the Founder and CEO of *The Art of Transparency, NFP* an organization with a mission to "focus on providing a positive platform of personal testimony to begin the Heal ONE Person, One City, ONE State, ONE Nation at a time through the Art of Transparency". Although passionate about teaching others about her journey which includes forgiving a father that wasn't, in her opinion, able to be the model man she had desperately needed as a young girl growing into womanhood, she continued to struggle with her inner feelings. Being able to convey these imbedded emotions is also comforting for her. Learning the *Art of Transparency* is equivalent to facing and being fully aware of who she is, her ability to candidly speak from the heart about real life issues and how to conquer life's trials is one of my greatest gifts.

Speaking to participants is a time for meaningful engagement. Time used to encourage, lead and offer real

The Birth to My Purpose
The Journey to Motherhood

life situations and results to enable listeners to truly understand and connect with her, not only as the speaker but to have empathy for the topic. One of the results that Mikkita obtains when speaking to audiences is her dynamic ability to ignite an awakening within those who hear her story. It allows them to realize and understand their issue more clearly, that she has been through similar situations and how they, too, can overcome the feelings and possible stagnations from its impact. These processes are all facilitated with audience in mind.

How beneficial it is to have the skill to ignite the path of change. Mikkita's niche is engaging her teen pregnancy and parenting audiences with realistic topics that help identify the issues and the teens' willingness to work towards resolutions. Her books, *The Letter From, the Invisible Daughter* as well as *The Cause and Effect of The Invisible Daughter*, talks about, among other topics, parenting a child that's different from the rest and her doubts of being a good mother. As she speaks candidly about her thoughts of suicide and being in unsafe relationships that included domestic violence; emotional, mental and physical, she creates and implements strategies to be used in the moment to begin healing processes for others. Most gatherings include hands-on activities. There's only room for results; a growth mindset. Mikkita continues to receive multiple invites to speak due this direct approach which call for peace and progress in the lives of others.

Mikkita along with her tour has scheduled and appeared for several presentations and speaking engagements, over the

The Birth to My Purpose
The Journey to Motherhood

last 3 years with heightened interest in each state. Moving forward there will be plans to host back-to-school events, expos, workshops and conferences on healing awareness.

www.mikkitamoore.com

info@mikkitamoore.com

The Birth to My Purpose
The Journey to Motherhood

It Was Never A Mistake

My journey to Motherhood started at the tender age of 11 years old…. No, I wasn't an actual mother, but I took care of my newborn nephew from birth until the age of one. I then had my own son at the age of 14 years old… And it was not a mistake…

Let me unpack that for you… A little of the back story is; At the age of 11 years old my older brother's girlfriend became pregnant; she was only 15 years old (she was 16 by the time my nephew was born). Her mother was not in support of her being a teenage mother. She was put out of the home, her and my nephew came to live with us (my mom, my brother and myself). She was in high school and a new mom without the help of her mom, my brother was running the street, hanging with his friends, she was alone a lot with my newborn nephew, all while trying to study and figure out this thing called life. In turn, I being a huge baby lover and the fact that he was a live-in baby, I took care of him daily. I fed him, played with him, changed his diapers, gave him baths, all of like he was a real live baby doll. Right after he turned a year old, my brother decided they would move to Memphis into their own place. Knowing that Memphis is an eight plus hour road trip, I knew it would be months before I would see my nephew again. I was crushed.

This same crushed feeling is a feeling that I knew all too well. It is the same crushed feeling that I had when I had to leave what I knew as my parents' home, to live with

The Birth to My Purpose
The Journey to Motherhood

my mom at 6 years old. The same crushed feeling I had when my mother left her abusive husband, and I never saw him again. The same crushed feeling that I had every time I would want my daddy and he didn't come or just wasn't there. This is the crushed feeling of complete abandonment, and I hated it!

All I ever wanted was love and acceptance. That is, it! I wanted real love from people that would *STAY* by my side and not leave me. I wanted real love from people because they loved me for me, and not for what they thought my mother or my brother or my father (for that matter) could give them. I just truly and honestly wanted to be loved. At age 11, I made in my mind that I would have my own baby! My Baby would be somebody that would love me no matter what. My baby would be somebody that would never leave me, no matter what. My baby would be *MINE... ALL MINE...*

Growing up my mother was in Nursing school so at times when she would study, I would get in the bed beside her and look, read and even try to memorize the things that I saw in her books. The one section that I loved the most was obstetrics. When she studied that subject, I made sure to run to her room to find out more about the female anatomy and how babies were born. I often wanted to be an Obstetrician as a little girl... until I found out how much school that was going to take.... I quickly changed my mind about that one.

When I said to myself that I wanted a baby, I figured there would be some pain at delivery, but I was

The Birth to My Purpose
The Journey to Motherhood

willing to do the pain to get my Baby. I also knew that I would have to have sex in order to get pregnant with my baby. Having had one very painful and horrifying sexual experience already, I honestly dd not want to do that again. However, the fact that the love I needed was more important, I no longer cared about the sexual pain either. All I wanted was LOVE... by any means necessary.

By the time I was 13 years old I was pregnant. A 13-year-old, 8th grader almost ready to graduate and go on to high school and pregnant… Wow... I am having a baby… A real live baby of my own. Because I was entering into high school pregnant, I was assigned a school for pregnant girls for my freshman year.

My first son was born January 9th 1992… I was 14 years old. The scariest and most amazing days of my life.

For the first couple months I was happy, I felt whole, I felt loved… However, that "feeling" didn't last very long; although I was happy, I was not fulfilled. Because I was a teen mom, my mother helped me out a lot from bathing my son to helping me at night with feedings. I once again felt as if I didn't have my baby to myself. By the time I was 15 years old, I was pregnant again. This pregnancy was not planned at all. It was more of a surprise. I was on birth control pills but I am sure I was not taking them correctly at all. I took them whenever I remembered, which may or may not have been every day.

When I found out that I was pregnant again, I hid it at first because in my mind I was going to "get rid of it".

The Birth to My Purpose
The Journey to Motherhood

Knowing that my mother was completely against abortions, I had no choice but to hide the pregnancy until I could figure out what I was really going to do about it. On one hand I wanted the baby but on the other hand I knew my mother would be so mad at me. My peers would laugh at me for having yet another baby. My father would probably disown me for a second baby before 21 years old. I just wasn't sure what to do.

    Not knowing what I truly wanted to do, I called the abortion clinic and made the appointment. I knew deep down that I never wanted an abortion but the feeling of disappointing my mother again was far greater than the feelings I had around just getting rid of the problem. The following week, when I got to the abortion clinic, I was completely scared, nervous and even more confused as to what I was really about to do, and how it would affect my body. I had heard horror stories from my peers about when abortions go wrong. I was so scared. The nurse called my name and took me to the back, in the back they took some blood to make sure I didn't have any infections, they had me undress from the waist down. I laid on the table for what felt like hours. The nurse comes back in to ask me "where is your mother, we need her signature". I was again in complete shock because my other of course was not there and furthermore had no clue I was pregnant or anywhere near an abortion clinic. The nurse said without your mother's signature because of your age we are unable to perform an abortion for you. I was devastated knowing that my mother would never come to sign off on such a

The Birth to My Purpose
The Journey to Motherhood

procedure. I was then told to get dressed and to reschedule when my mother could stay with me to sign the consent.

I quickly got dressed and went home. The bus ride home, I cried and cried, not because I was sad that I couldn't get the abortion, but because I knew, that I had no choice but to tell my mother that I was pregnant. I knew she would be extremely disappointed in me again, which is something that I never wanted to experience again. When I got home my brother had already called my mother to tell her that I pregnant. To back up just a little bit, when I found out that I was pregnant, I confided in my brother's girlfriend (which was like my big sister) that I was pregnant and that I was scared to get an abortion. She told me that I should just tell my mom and get it over with, she said, yeah, she may be mad for a little while but she would eventually be okay with it and life would be go on just fine again. Of course, I was not trying to hear what she was saying at the time. So, when my brother found out that I had gone to the abortion clinic in his way of stopping me, he told our mother that I was pregnant, her response was "I know that already". I was completely shocked that she was so calm about it. She gave me her this is not the life I wanted for you speech but she was nothing like I had imagined in my head.

August 30th, 1993, three weeks before my 16th birthday, I gave birth to my second child, my daughter, she was 7 pounds even and 19 inches long. She was beautiful and once again, she was all mine. I once again felt like I was complete, I was a mother of two and a Junior in High

The Birth to My Purpose
The Journey to Motherhood

School, life was great. Or at least it was for the moment. I was a teenage mom of two, an honor roll student, and still knew nothing about real love or what real love looked or felt like.

As a teenage mother I did not allow that to hinder me at all. I graduated my junior year of high school with honors. I went on to have three more children a few years later. I am a mother of five, my children are now ages 28, 27, 21, 16, and 9, all of them are doing well. The older two children have children of their own, making me a grandmother of 8. I truly enjoy being a grandmother almost more than I enjoyed being a mother.

My journey to motherhood wasn't a path that I would ever want my children to take, however, I do know that, it's not the worst thing that could have happen to me. Yes, my life was a little harder than my peers in the aspect of I couldn't go to the after-school games and/or functions because I had to go home and be a mother but I wouldn't change any of it even if I could. My children are my world and I love them more than I could have ever imagined. Whatever your journey is or will be, my advice is to embrace it and truly love on yourself through your journey to motherhood.

The Birth to My Purpose
The Journey to Motherhood

Chapter Two

A Parent That Didn't Really Know How to Parent?

Paula Kendrick

The Birth to My Purpose
The Journey to Motherhood

Paula Kendrick a woman who perseveres each and every day. She is a mother of four daughters with various roles; She host and produces her own live stream and podcast giving encouraging words of inspiration and long with much laughter to bless others by saying "Continually Let Your Light Shine" and "Be Blessed and be a Blessing". Kendrick is a true servant at heart for God.

Author Paula Kendrick

http://amazon.com/author/paulakendrick

The Birth to My Purpose
The Journey to Motherhood

A Parent That Didn't Really Know How to Parent?

I have always wanted to be a mom with three kids since I was about 7 years old. Can you believe that someone that young wanted to be a mother? I used to say that I was going to have two boys and one girl. I always wanted my first born to be a boy because he could be the protector over his sister(s). Well, I actually ended up having three girls and they were truly a handful but a blessing. I always thought that having daughters would be easy because you could dress them up in pretty little dresses with the bows and barrettes. I know that my mom kept me in the cute little dresses with the ruffle panties and she never let me get dirty. That was just taboo to let your daughter get dirty right (lol). You never think that your children will eventually grow up with a mind of their own, with their own attitude and feelings. Parenting stages of babies, infants up to teenage years were pretty kosher without any worries or problems because as mothers, you can give them a look, which lets them know you mean business. Mothers also carry a high pitch in our voice, which they can decipher that something is going on. When they are in their terrible twos, they have the temper tantrums and then you wonder what happened to the sweet little child that you brought home from the hospital. Once you get over that hump then you come into teenage adolescent stage and boy you want to pull all of your hair out.

The Birth to My Purpose
The Journey to Motherhood

     This is when they start having the mood swings and the bad behavior which could be attributed to hormones or just the company in which they keep. Either way you just want to go somewhere and scream at the top of your lungs. It is funny with siblings because they are each other's first friends in the beginning, they know each other from the inside and out. It is so weird that you have children who grow up together in the same household and yet they are totally different. I will discuss my children in sequence from the eldest to the youngest. My first born whom I will call Tameka has always been the prissy type. She played with the dolls, always wanting to dress up, put on the makeup, she was like the mommy to her baby dolls and stuffed animals. She was the girlie girl out of the bunch, which means she never really wanted to get dirty, she was such a neat freak. To this day she is still a neat freak and doesn't like anything out of place or to get dirty. She started early with the eye rolling and being defiant. I truly lost count on the many times she got grounded or got her cell phone taken away for her disrespectful behavior. Now I did have to physically disciple her but it was not too often because taking her cell phone from her was as though you had stabbed her or something. She is now an adult with an undergrad as well as a graduate degree under her belt and still striving. I look back at her now in astonishment. I felt like I was hard on her at times because I had to stay on her constantly about her behavior.

     What made me realize that I was totally not a bad mom, she happened to write me a letter, it was so passionate, heartfelt and appreciative. She said she didn't think I was mean, but she felt that I didn't listen to her or understand her. She also stated in the letter that she

The Birth to My Purpose
The Journey to Motherhood

appreciated me looking out for her because she knew that I loved her and I was doing it out of love. Even when we think our children are not listening to us, we get confirmation that they are.

My second daughter whom I will call Lillian, was a hand full at its best. She has always been the real spunky sassy one out of the bunch. She was also the quietest and well reserved one who kept to herself. I remember parenting her, it was very difficult. She was more defiant and just seemed to do things because she wanted to or felt like it. You always hear that the middle child has that middle child syndrome and boy I surely felt like she did. There were several instances where we constantly stayed into verbal altercations, she got a lot of whooping's as a child. I had gotten to the point, where I was fed up with her, I didn't know anything else to do but literally ask her to leave. Asking her to leave nicely was like the PG version of a movie, if we were doing a movie scene. I couldn't believe it myself, that I was putting my own child out of my house, but I did not know of any other way. When you have an almost adult (who would have been 17 years old) trying to tell you what they are and are not going to do, living in your house you tend to lose focus. It was so hard watching her leave, but I had to stay firm. I could not let her disrespect me or my home, now could I?

Of course, I could not, because God tells us in Ephesians 6:1-2 Children, obey your parents in the Lord, for this is right. 2 "Honor your father and mother"- which is the first commandment with a promise NIV. Being responsible for other human beings is a hard task in itself. Who knew that a little bundle of joy would have a

The Birth to My Purpose
The Journey to Motherhood

personality out of this world and at times is nothing like you? Grown people have to be on their own, with responsibilities of their own, but when you have not reached adulthood, as the world sees it at the ripe age of 20 then what is one to do? When you are on a job and you behave a certain way, you will be reprimanded in some way by a verbal warning. If it gets out of hand then you are terminated. This is exactly what happened to her for not following the rules that had been laid before her. While she was gone, she did write me a sweet letter, explaining how she felt. I think I would have been in a strait jacket in the crazy house, because, I felt like I was bad at parenting her as well. The letter that Lillian wrote stated, she wanted to say so much but didn't know where to begin. She stated how protective I was over them; monitoring what they watched and who they hung out with. She even stated that over the years there were times where she knew we couldn't stand one another or get along. She summed up the letter by thanking me for looking out for her, even when she didn't think she needed it, she thanked me for letting her fall, so she could learn from her mistakes. She thanked me for putting up with her for 18 years and loving her no matter what. I don't think I cried so much in my life, as I did from reading her letter… it touched me so much.

My third daughter (baby girl) whom we will call Kay-Kay, started out being mean and looking at people sideways when she was about 5 years old. She made faces, looking at everyone crazy, she always had this scowl on her face. She was actually a happy baby, parenting her was far easier than the other two I truly tell you. She did not go through her adolescent stage until she was actually grown about 18 years of age or so.

The Birth to My Purpose
The Journey to Motherhood

I used to think that she saw how much trouble her sisters got into, and maybe she figured it out that life would be much smoother if she did what was asked of her. She is like the visionary of the family. She makes you reflect on your flaws, imperfections and calls you out on them. She makes you take a look at your life, making you feel as if you will do anything needed to change your ways. I may have had to physically punish her two or three times, which is far and few compared to her siblings. She would actually come talk to me and tell me if she got into trouble in school or something, before I got the phone call or found out about it. I guess you could say she knew how to work the system (lol).

Now my birth to my purpose; it started out as me being adopted and making sure that my children would have the necessary love that they needed, but yet they didn't have me fully. I struggled with wanting to keep my kids safe, wanting to do everything humanly possible to make sure they had what they needed. When my children were defiant and disrespectful it would always trigger me. I would revert back to that little child. A child who needed her mom's love as well as the mom who would do everything necessary to gain the respect, that was warranted and expected of and from them. When I got the eye roll, neck roll, the un-harmonious words then it made me mad. How dare a child, let alone my own child disrespect me? Parenting does not come with a manual, which sometimes I wish it would have because it would have saved so much time and heartache. You see parents talking about their kids and they never gave them grief, you wonder what happened on your pathway of parenting, that you were catching hell in your household. First, you have

The Birth to My Purpose
The Journey to Motherhood

to forgive yourself because you only did and made the decisions that you thought was right at the time.

Once, I stopped feeling sorry for myself, only then was I able to heal in some areas that I needed to be healed in. We have all said things we did not mean, knowing how words can truly hurt us. We have to apologize to ourselves for what was said and we have to forgive others for what was said to us. I would not change the way I disciplined my children in any way, because I now see the fruits which sprung forth from the parenting that was done. I see that my children and I do have a good relationship now, despite the previous paths taken. As mothers, we just have to rely more on God for guidance. God is there in all of our steps, guiding us, sometimes we let him stay silent and dormant but we need him in all areas of our lives and our children's lives. Looking back, I never knew that the pain that transpired in their lives nor in mine would lead to My Purpose. My Purpose to tell the story that no one, not even myself is exempt from pain. Stop trying to be perfect because we are not in any way, shape, form or fashion. Take responsibility for the pain that you have caused, whether physical or verbal and do things to rectify the situation. Persons and situations can heal only if you put forth the effort and determination to do so. My purpose are the three girls that I gave birth to and still look out for even though they are grown. The process of having them (heartburn, morning sickness, stretch marks, colic, late night feedings) is well worth the end result of giving birth to them. These young ladies have taught me that discipline, boundaries and rules are a part of parenting. To be successful in life you need all of these things. Parents have to realize also that we have to take time for ourselves to recoup to be effective parents. Learn to keep our emotions and feelings in check to not make our children feel unworthy. Show that we love them and are here for them in case they need us. Just know that as parents we will fail and fall multiple times but to not wallow in it, or feel bad for the decisions that we made regarding our family.

The Birth to My Purpose
The Journey to Motherhood

The Birth to My Purpose
The Journey to Motherhood

Chapter Three

'Steels Toes and Stilettos': Reflections of a Military Mom

Dr. Stacy L Henderson

The Birth to My Purpose
The Journey to Motherhood

Dr. Stacy L. Henderson, a native of Savannah, Georgia, is a highly decorated retired Naval Officer with over 25 years of military service and experience. She is a Christian Educator, Inspirational Speaker, Businesswoman and an International Best-Selling Author. She speaks four languages and has publications in more than 40 language translations - two of which are in the White House Library. Her *Stacy's Stocking Stuffers* Christmas Charity has provided toys, meals, coats, clothing and monetary support for families around the world since 1991.

Stacy has spent much of her life overcoming challenges. Her *'Survival Journal'* chronicles her trauma and triumph over childhood sexual assault and domestic abuse as an adult. In it, she shares first-hand accounts while raising awareness of domestic violence. *'Fair Winds And Following Seas'* is a letter written to her Navy Shipmates during the recovery and rehabilitation process after a near fatal domestic incident. The letter was later recreated as a Public Service Announcement (MarcMann Productions, Chicago) and is widely used in Military Domestic Violence training sessions. Her other military-themed PSAs based on her experiences include: *'Introducing Stacy L. Henderson: The Woman Behind the Uniform'*; *'The Sailor on the Pier'* and *'The War At Home.'* Her personal story of triumph over tragedy was featured in Military One Source Magazine, Great Lakes Bulletin and multiple other Media

The Birth to My Purpose
The Journey to Motherhood

Outlets. An active Member of the National Coalition Against Domestic Violence (NCADV), Stacy is an avid supporter of abuse victims, survivors, and their loved ones. She still supports the programs at the Shelter where she and her children once resided. The facility was instrumental in their safe escape from an abusive environment. With violence on the rise among our youth, she also provides age-appropriate anti-bullying training to young adults. She testified at Congressional Hearings in efforts to get tougher abuse perpetrator laws passed during the President Clinton and President Obama Administrations (Violence Against Women Act).

Stacy has worked on projects with Paramount Motion Pictures, *Lifetime* Television, BET, TV One, Mary Kay Domestic Violence Foundation, Dr. Iyanla Vanzant (OWN Network) and the late, great Dr. Maya Angelou. She has been featured in numerous Media outlets including Black Enterprise Magazine; Savannah Herald; Savannah Tribune; Chicago Defender; Chicago Access Network TV, *Unveil'D* Celebrity News Magazine, and the Steve Harvey, Michael Baisden and Tom Joyner Radio Shows. Her Professional Affiliations include: National Baptist Convention, USA, Inc.; Gullah Geechee Sea Island Coalition; *Spirit of Excellence* Business Awards (Stellar Productions); 'Toots for Books' Literacy Foundation; Professional Woman Network; National Women Veterans United; Veterans of Foreign Wars (VFW); Frank Callen Boys and Girls Club Alumni Association and Delta Sigma Theta Sorority, Inc. Her personal accolades include Outstanding Georgia Citizen, Two (2) Guinness World Records, a BET *Her*

The Birth to My Purpose
The Journey to Motherhood

Humanitarian Award, Reaching Back Foundation Phenomenal Woman Award, NCADV 2020 *Power Up, Survivor Activist Award,* 'Keys to the City' for Eight (8) United States locales and countless other Military and Civilian Awards and Commendations.

Stacy shares her life experiences and relies on faith-based doctrines to motivate and inspire others to achieve their best mental, physical and spiritual health. She has Degrees in Education, Health Services Management, Christian Leadership and Business Administration. A Proverbs 31 Woman, she utilizes her Spiritual Gifts to glorify God and edify His people. She is a loving Wife, loving Grandmother and proud mother of two adult children, KeiSha and William. They are blessed to be members of a beautiful 'Blended and Extended' Family. To God be the Glory!

The Birth to My Purpose
The Journey to Motherhood

'Steels Toes and Stilettos': Reflections of a Military Mom

Today, I am sitting here dining with my children, KeiSha and William, at our favorite Metro-Atlanta, Georgia Cafe', appropriately named *Peaches' Place*. It is a nice, relaxing hang out spot with a laid-back family atmosphere. The faint scent of lemons, peaches, lavender and vanilla surrounds us as we sit on the outdoor patio, soaking up the Georgia sun, over a Saturday mid-morning brunch. The Chef, lovingly known as 'Chef WB', is an amazing Cook and his signature dish is Lobster Casttanine. Out of all of the meals he prepares - that one has always been my absolute favorite. While sharing laughs over great food and drinks, my mind slowly drifted and wandered to days long past. A time when life's challenges and family struggles tested our faith. Nevertheless, by the Grace of God, we made it.

While reminiscing with KeiSha and William about our travels, our lives and what the future holds...it made me a little sad. They were raised as 'Military Brats' - a term of endearment used in the United States to identify the child or children of a parent or parents serving full-time in the United States Armed Forces, whether current or former. Both of my children had traveled the world, made many friends, and were exposed to various cultures and languages. As exciting and adventurous as it sounds, living such a lifestyle has its downsides. For example, making friends was easy but staying connected sometimes proved difficult - especially with families relocating every two to

The Birth to My Purpose
The Journey to Motherhood

three years. My children changed schools frequently and school year calendars varied based on our location. Another concern was a disconnection from our family and friends. While moving from state to state and country to country, we settled into a routine and became dependent on each other. And although we were family...we had become part of the 'Navy Family.' We subscribed to the notion that *'Home is where the Navy sends us.'*

As our conversation continued, I looked into KeiSha's eyes and saw so much of myself when I was younger. Her bubbly personality, sweetness and compassion for others always delighted me. Her physical features are stunning. She is very beautiful, dark skinned and has the whitest and brightest smile imaginable. Her father and I were very young and inexperienced when she was conceived. We were good friends and dated during our Junior Year in High School. We loved each other in a sweet teenage way. We both worked part-time jobs while in school and we had big plans for our lives. KeiSha's father, Keith, wanted to own his own business someday and I planned to join the military. Being teenage parents was not in our plans. We tried to make our relationship work and build a strong family unit but at our age, we were unprepared. We had few resources of our own and needed a lot of help from both of our families. The stress of teen parenting was overwhelming at times. So much so that we eventually went our separate ways. And, one day...there I was...an unwed teenage Mother.

The Birth to My Purpose
The Journey to Motherhood

Entering my Senior Year of High School, I was unsure of myself, uncertain about life and I had little confidence that I could raise a child on my own. By that time, I was working at KFC and it was very difficult to go to school and work a full-time job. My mother had suggested that maybe I should take a year off from school, adjust to motherhood and go back to school later. That was not what I had in mind. I wanted to graduate with my friends, and I knew that if I stopped going to school it would be hard to start back up again - especially with a baby. I worked on adjusting my future plans because they now included KeiSha.

Eventually my school and work schedule took a toll on me physically, emotionally and mentally. I was stressed but I needed to have a solid future for KeiSha and I. Although Keith and I had parted ways, he visited us often. He also worked a full-time job while also struggling to finish school.

One day, Military Recruiters came to visit the students at my High School. After hearing the various Career Options, they spoke about, I signed up to take the Armed Services Vocational Aptitude Battery (ASVAB) Test. Within a week of their visit, I had taken the ASVAB, scored very high on it, and started processing my application for the U. S. Navy's Delayed Entry Program (DEP) so I could start my military career right after High School. I developed a Dependent Care Plan for KeiSha since I was a single parent and would need to arrange reliable care for her in my absence. And, since I had

The Birth to My Purpose
The Journey to Motherhood

completed four years of JROTC in Middle and High School, I qualified to enlist as an E-3 - or Seaman - since I was joining the Navy. My career choice was Dental Technician (DT).

As time went on, KeiSha's father and I co-parented as best we could but we barely saw each other. As our High School Graduation day was approaching, my Enlistment date was delayed, so I put my backup plan into action: I applied to a few colleges and filled out scholarship applications. I wanted to keep moving forward with my life. As God would have it, I was accepted to Savannah State College (now University) - an HBCU in my hometown. I was awarded several Academic Scholarships and Grants. So, there would be no cost for my education.

On graduation day, I strutted excitedly across the stage at the Savannah Civic Center, shook hands with the school officials and received my Diploma, walked off the stage and over to my Mother. I took KeiSha from her arms, kissed her on both cheeks and held her tight. I then returned to my seat to rejoin my classmates, placed my daughter on my lap, and I sat there with tears of joy streaming down my face. Our future looked bright. Not only was I a Navy Seaman BUT a Graduate of the Alfred Ely Beach High School Class of 1989. I was SO proud that I had earned my High School Diploma!

My first day at Savannah State was refreshing. I was still working full time but after graduating High School I took a week off from work just to relax, and spend time with KeiSha. I was now working at Popeye's on M. L.

The Birth to My Purpose
The Journey to Motherhood

King, Jr. Boulevard. It was a good job and a few of my friends worked there - which made it enjoyable. It was there that I met my future husband, Willie. We had known each other most of our lives, our parents were friends and our families were long time acquaintances. Sure, we always were in each other's space but not romantically. Little did we know that we were in the perfect time and place for a new romance.

We dated while I attended Savannah State and worked at Popeyes. After about six months into our relationship, he met KeiSha and the two of them connected instantly. I was pleased because her father and I had both moved on with our lives. In fact, he had moved away from Savannah to a nearby town. We did not see or hear from him too often after he moved away. I had very strong feelings for Willie and I wanted to pace myself this time. I wanted things to be good for all of us.

Near the end of my Freshman year of college, I prepared to enter the Navy. And, in August 1991, I went to Basic Training in Orlando, Florida. Willie and my Mother took care of KeiSha while I was in training and afterwards, Willie and I were married in a huge, elaborate, fairytale church wedding. It was the wedding I had dreamed about since I was a little girl. Our families, friends and loved ones were there. And, KeiSha was a beautiful Flower Girl. She looked so proud standing there with me and Willie. We were in love and we were a family. *It was magical!*

After Willie and I wed, went on our Honeymoon and returned home, we had some adjustments to make. I

The Birth to My Purpose
The Journey to Motherhood

went to San Diego, California for Dental Technician Apprentice School. He and KeiSha remained in Savannah until after I completed my studies. Going to San Diego without Willie and KeiSha was heartbreaking but I needed to complete my training program.

So, as graduation day approached, I looked at the list of available locations - most of them were overseas - and the best option for us appeared to be San Diego, California. I called Willie, read him the list and asked what he thought. We discussed it and agreed that San Diego was our choice. A few months later, he and KeiSha joined me in San Diego. We moved into a nice two-bedroom apartment and started our 'Navy Life' together.

As time went on, I noticed that I was slowly being haunted by my past. Recurring nightmares and physical illness started to consume me. I started having thoughts of shame about the molestation I endured as a child. As much as I loved Willie, I was ashamed to express my embarrassment about my body image as a result of my childhood trauma. I was confused and I started resenting myself for being '*damaged.*' I eventually shared as much as I could but so much of it was too painful to relive and I just could not find the courage to be completely vulnerable.

After three years of marriage, Willie and I had a son who we named William Robert. William, after Willie's maternal grandfather and Robert after my father. Both men had passed on but our son's name represented both of their strength and character. And, the last name 'Brown' is one

The Birth to My Purpose
The Journey to Motherhood

of integrity. After William's birth, things changed drastically. I felt disconnected from my husband and children. They were like strangers to me, and, some days, I didn't even know who I was. Those feelings persisted for months. Then...one day...I woke up and decided to walk away from my family because I was afraid that if I did not leave them, I would lose them. So, I embarked on a path of healing and recovery...alone. It took years for me to heal from Postpartum depression, along with a myriad of other childhood trauma and abuse. Through it all, I knew that hope was essential for healing, which would lead to restoration.

We were mid-way through our meal when we heard an old familiar whistling sound coming from the kitchen as 'Chef WB' was signaling us to get back to work. He jokingly reminded KeiSha and I that as the Co-Owners of the establishment, we should be working, not brunching. We laughed as he smiled at us. We smiled back at him and I nodded my head in an up and down 'Yes' motion. KeiSha and I took the hint, freshened up and returned to work. William, who was visiting us, along with his family, from his Navy Duty Station in Japan, remained at the table waiting for his father to join him. Willie, lovingly known as 'Chef WB', removed his apron, freshened up and joined William at the table.

I stood in the kitchen watching two of the most important men in my life as they sat at the table on the patio, enjoying their conversation. It had been years since I saw the two of them together like that. Despite the

The Birth to My Purpose
The Journey to Motherhood

challenges that life put before us, Willie has always been a caring friend, a great provider and a devoted family man. I will always love and admire him for that. As I was on my healing journey, while serving in the Navy, the children spent much of their time with me after Willie had relocated and settled down outside of Atlanta. They spent some summers with him and when I deployed at sea, he took care of them. He wanted us all to relocate to the Atlanta area together as a family, but the emotional wounds of my past had me convinced that I was not 'good enough' to be a good wife or a decent mother. I had a lot of issues to work through and I wanted to get healthy for me and for my family. Not only did God heal my wounds, He blessed me by restoring my family. William is very much like his father: loving, protective, caring, intelligent, and a great cook. KeiSha is a 'Daddy's Girl' who has the love of her father, Keith, and her 'Bonus Dad,' Willie. She is bright, beautiful, compassionate and her love of children is heartwarming.

I was startled by the sounds of loud talking and laughter as a large group of my 'Blended and Extended' Family members arrived at *Peaches' Place.* I smiled through my tears and greeted everyone as they headed to the patio to join Willie and William. KeiSha removed her apron, blew me a kiss, and went to join the others on the patio when she noticed that her father, Keith, was with the group. Our Staff happily accommodated everyone that was in *Peaches' Place* that afternoon - restaurant patrons and family, too. There were husbands and wives, parents and grandparents, children and grandchildren, aunts, uncles and

The Birth to My Purpose
The Journey to Motherhood

cousins - all talking, laughing and loving each other. It warmed my heart to see everyone together. I stood there with tears in my eyes as I said to myself, *"Family is love and love is family. Thank you, Lord, for such a blessing!"*

Before anyone noticed me crying, I rushed into the ladies' restroom, locked the door and cried for a good five minutes. I was overcome with so much love and deep emotion that I could barely breathe. Once I caught my breath, I splashed cold water on my face, dried it with a fresh peach-scented towel, pulled myself together and went back to work. I helped serve food and drinks and visited with my family every chance I got. The whole place was buzzing with excitement. Family is a treasure and mine is priceless.

So, whether I am wearing Steel Toes or Stilettos, this is one 'Military Mom' who enjoys Motherhood. Thanks to KeiSha and William, I have had an abundance of life experiences that I would not trade for anything in this world. Sure, we had our share of good days and bad days. But, we also shared years of happiness, tears of joy, and a lifetime of love. My journey to Motherhood has been challenging yet fulfilling. Despite the trials and tribulations, we endured, unconditional love conquers all. My children are blessings and priceless gifts from God. I am honored to be their Mother. To God Be the Glory!

The Birth to My Purpose
The Journey to Motherhood

The Birth to My Purpose
The Journey to Motherhood

Chapter Four

Sometimes You Have to Fight

Latonya Willett

The Birth to My Purpose
The Journey to Motherhood

Latonya Brown Willett, a wife of 25 years, mother of 4, financial analyst, entrepreneur, motivational speaker, and Evangelist. Latonya was born on the Westside of Chicago. She's the next to youngest of 4 children. At a very early age, (4 years old) Latonya always had a caring heart for others. She would help others as much as she could by giving of her time, money, toys, and anything else she had to give.

As Latonya became older, she still had a caring spirit, but ran into life along the way. By the age of 15, she had her first child and by the time she was 17 she had her second child. While struggling to keep up her grades and take care of 2 children with the support of only her older sister, her second child would eventually die at the age of 4 months old on Mother's Day from SIDS. Only by the grace of God did Latonya navigate her way through depression, suicide attempts and more, to be able to care for her older son.

4 months after the death of her son, she met the man that would later become her husband. They have 2 sons together and 2 grandsons, one from the oldest and 1 from the middle son.

Latonya has a background in Nursing and Science. Latonya is now and has been a Financial Analyst, for the past 18

The Birth to My Purpose
The Journey to Motherhood

years, known as The Money Lady. She analyzes and presents budget plans, investment ideas, as well as provide insurance options. Latonya has won many awards associated with the work she does for her clients, and has been recognized and celebrated as one of the "100 Black Queens of Chicago". She's the Outreach Director of her church as well as an ordained Evangelist, has her own Non-Profit called "Blessings From Heaven". She also helps her 20-year-old son run both of his businesses, Dance Characters and BopKing Larry Entertainment. The 2 of them travel to schools teaching the children about how money works and how they can become business owner's themselves. Latonya is a real Comeback Queen with a demonstrated wealth of knowledge of life's hardships, overcoming obstacles, business, wealth creation, and legacy building.

To contact Latonya Willett, you can reach her by email at LatonyaWillett@yahoo.com

The Birth to My Purpose
The Journey to Motherhood

Sometimes You Have to Fight

My journey to motherhood was very unorthodox. I became a mother at an early age. I became a mother at the age of 14. I didn't know all the ins and outs of getting pregnant, and I trusted the person I was with to not get me pregnant, but later, I would find out that, that was his main focus. Once I found out I was pregnant, I had to run away from home to keep my baby because my mother wanted me to have an abortion. I hid out for a couple of weeks. I called my sister every night to let her know I was alright, but I was not coming home until I knew I could keep my baby. Once I had my baby, I fell in love with him. He was such a good baby. He would only wake up during the night if he needed to be changed, after that, he would go back to sleep. I would just hold him, look at him, kiss him and tell him how much I loved him. My mother would look at me and say that I must have tried to get pregnant on purpose, simply because I was showing my baby some love. I never understood that.

    I would have my next child with the same guy when I was 17 years old. I kept the fact that I was pregnant a secret for as long as I could. I knew my mother would want me to have an abortion with this one too. I was not doing that. Once she found out, she had my sister take me to the abortion clinic. They said I was too far long, so they would have to do surgery and it would cost a lot more money. I was so glad. That meant that I would be able to have my baby. He was such a good baby. He would just lay in the

The Birth to My Purpose
The Journey to Motherhood

bed and look at the ceiling the entire time. If you held him too long, he would cry for you to put him down.

I went to school; I worked hard to get good grades and hold down a job to take care of my babies. Although, it was incredibly stressful, I was determined to get through school and take care of my babies. Until, one day on Mother's Day in 1993. DeAndre was only 4 months old. He went to sleep and never awakened. He died from S.I.D.S., Sudden Infant Death Syndrome. I was very depressed after his passing. I had to go through a lot of prayer and counseling to get better. I just did not want to live anymore. The death of a child is just not natural. The children are supposed to bury the parents, not the other way around. That was too catastrophic for a 17-year-old to handle.

Although, we were not together at the time, my children's father ended up in jail. I was so depressed that I went from being a straight A student to being a straight F student. I went from living life to not wanting to live at all. I attempted to take my life at least 3 times. That was a very dark time for me. Out of every bad situation, there does come some good. I did not know that 4 months later I would meet the man that I would later call my husband. It was just a fluke that I met him. I was getting clothes from home for the next day to go to work. My mother told me to get my hair done by the girl that lived downstairs. While I was there, he came by with his baby's mother to get her hair done. They were not together either, he was doing her a favor. I made sure of that. I did not want to be the cause of someone breaking up. I even tried to talk him into

The Birth to My Purpose
The Journey to Motherhood

getting back with her the entire first 2 weeks that we would talk. I believe in couples and families making it work if they can.

I really did not think it would last, because I had never been with anyone tall before. All my boyfriends had been short or my height. This was new to me. Turns out we hit it off very well. Even though, he was older than me, we were growing together. We were always asked by everyone when we would have children. As soon as you get married, people expect you to get pregnant as soon as possible. I wanted to wait to have children. I felt, he had a son already and so did I, so there was no reason to rush into having children. Soon, he would begin to want a child. I held off for as long as I could. Four years later, I would give birth to our first son together, Larry Willett Jr.

I had always been guided before on how I should discipline my child, because I didn't know any better at the time. What I should do for him, or not do for him. While the guidance was needed, at times it wasn't always the best information. I did not have to worry about someone hovering over me while I showered him with love, making me feel guilty because I was loving my baby. Oh my God! It was just so peaceful, tranquil, and everything I wanted it to be. He was my fresh start. This was my chance to get it right. I wanted Larry to have everything that I could not give his brothers that came before him. He had a real father, not just a sperm donor. We were married. He was planned. There was no judgement, just love for our child and one another. I bought all the pictures and little trinkets

The Birth to My Purpose
The Journey to Motherhood

from when they take the baby's picture in the hospital. I bought all the cute little boy clothes and blankets to match. I breastfed all my children. I would just sit and talk and coo with him for hours. I was in bliss. He was an incredibly good baby. I had trained myself to be up through the middle of the night, thinking that he would keep me up, but he didn't. He slept through the night.

Everything was great, until they sent me home from the hospital with a monitor on my baby. They gave me this, because they said baby's that die from S.I.D.S. usually have a sibling die from SIDS right after. Needless to say, I was a nervous wreck. I was up all-night checking to see if my baby was breathing. Checking every little beep, the monitor made if he turned a certain way in his crib. To make matters worse, he developed asthma. His asthma was so chronic, there were times when my husband would be rushing us to the hospital, or we'd be in the ambulance and my baby would seem to die in my arm's because he would stop breathing. I would continue to pat him and breath for him. I never told him this, but just the other day (Nov. 25, 2020) while we were talking, he told me he remembers dying in my arms and coming back to life. I do not know how he knows that he was only a few months old at the time. He is now 21. I used to take him to church, take him to anyone I knew who believed in God and had power and conviction to pray for him. I had to give him six different medicines, three times a day, at different times of the day. I was practically giving my baby medicine all day every day. We were back and forth between the nebulizer machine and other liquids. I was so afraid that I was going to lose

The Birth to My Purpose
The Journey to Motherhood

another child. That is the most horrible feeling in the world that a mother could ever have. I do not wish that on my worst enemy.

After many years, we finally got past that situation, to the point where he was able to run track, play basketball and do other sports just like the other children. People would ask me, why I was letting him play sports since he had asthma. I told them, first of all, God has healed him and secondly, if you keep a child sitting still, they will not have the chance to build up their lung capacity. Our lungs are like muscles, we must exercise them for them to work at a higher capacity. If we don't then we run the risk of handicapping them. There were still times when he would have a flare up whenever the weather changed; I would always keep the nebulizer machine ready for those times. There was one time, when he had a mild flare up, but he was out of medicine. It just so happened to be at the time of his doctor's appointment. The doctor prescribed the medicine so all we had to do was go to our pharmacy to pick it up. Well, let's just say some people should not have important jobs. The pharmacist continued to tell me that my insurance was having an issue and that she could not fill the prescription. I tried to talk to her and walk her through it because this happened before. She did not want to talk to me. It got so bad that I really had to get irate and have the store manager go to the back with me so that I could show him how to input the insurance. Well, by that time, he had been out of his medicine for too long. We walked out to the parking lot to get in the car and passed by a man that was smoking. That was it! I had to rush my child, to the ER. At

The Birth to My Purpose
The Journey to Motherhood

that time, he was 16 or 17 years old. It was so bad that they had to shoot him three times with epinephrine. The doctors were hysterical. They were hysterical because he has never had to have an epi shot before and usually for people who do need them will comply after the first one. Even though I was sitting in the chair calm praying knowing that God was in control, the reactions of the doctors made him nervous. You could see his heart beating out of his chest. I stood over him, placed my hand on his heart and told him he was going to be fine. I prayed so that he could hear me and continued to tell him he would be alright, and he began to comply with the medicine. Needless to say, I sued that pharmacy for hurting my baby.

Since all of that, he now has his own company, Dance Character's, where all he does is dance and entertain children. He works as an independent contractor with a band for weddings as a dancer entertainer. He also works as an independent contractor with a group that does celebrity impersonations.

Now, onto my last little pea in the pod. He's a very well-rounded little guy. I tell my sons all the time, that he is a mixture of them both. Just trying to find his way through it all. He loves his brothers very much. Right now, we are going through the Covid-19 pandemic. It is starting to take a little bit of a toll on him, because he is so used to seeing and interacting with his friends and now, he is unable to. His brother tries to spend as much time with him as he can. They make dance video's together and ride around in the car. Now, the Illinois school systems are in the works of

The Birth to My Purpose
The Journey to Motherhood

trying to get the children back in school, even though the cases are rising. It has even been shown that school's that have opened have almost fifty percent new cases and higher. It is like sending the children to slaughter to me. I just cannot do it. So, the fight continues. I will keep my child home until it is safe.

So, as you can see, my journey to motherhood has been a struggle and fight all my life. It has been a fight to bring life to my children and it has been a fight to keep the life of my children. I will continue to fight for my children's life as well as speak life into them. God gave them to me, so I must have good stewardship over them. I must give life, protect their life, speak life, and help them to have a flourishing life. I help them in every area they need me to. Whether it is in school, life, or giving them the courage and knowledge that they need to start a business and be successful in it. Sometimes you just need encouragement to make it through the day. Especially with them being young black men, I cannot slack at all in my teaching, encouraging, pushing, strengthening, education, etc. I must do my part as their mother. If I don't nurture and teach them, who else will? The earth, universe, world, and system are designed to kill them before they can even make it out of the womb. It will not happen on my watch, if I have anything to say about it. This is my journey to motherhood.

The Birth to My Purpose
The Journey to Motherhood

Chapter Five

Unplanned... But Purpose Was Birthed

Yolanda Givens

The Birth to My Purpose
The Journey to Motherhood

Yolanda Givens is a Chicago native but lived most of her life (30 plus years) in Los Angeles. While she now embraces and resides in Chicago, she still considers herself a California Girl.

This University of California, Irvine alumna began her nonprofit career in 1995. She was one of the key leaders in California's Statewide Initiative to Reduce Youth Violence during the later 90s and early 2000s and received several awards and recognitions for her commitment to making a difference in the lives of children and families.

It was 2004 when Yolanda transitioned to higher education. She spent five years at Loyola Marymount University (LMU) where her professionalism, work ethics, contributions and leadership led to the honor of receiving an honorary membership for Kappa Delta Pi awarded by LMU's Graduate School of Education. She returned to her place of birth in 2009 and worked at Loyola University of Chicago (LUC) but after 3 years, made the decision to leave LUC and reconnect to the nonprofit world and pursue her longtime dream of entrepreneurship.

Yolanda is the co-owner of BFF Management, a boutique firm that provides consulting and management in the areas of education and nonprofit.

She is one of the owners of TGP (Thycke Girl Productions), a theater and entertainment production company launched in 2017 with its first original play, Diary

The Birth to My Purpose
The Journey to Motherhood

of Thykce Girl that received raved reviews. Yolanda has been performing since she was young. She has received professional coaching and training in acting, vocals and dance from some of the best in Los Angeles.

Finally, Yolanda is one of the leading forces behind the Curve Appeal Chicago, a movement and sisterhood, now a 501c3 organization that has had a positive impacted the lives of women and girls for 9 years. In 2018, Yolanda received a monetary award from Chicago Community Trust to implement a women's mental health and wellness campaign.

Yolanda has trained, coached, supervised, and mentored numerous individuals in various capacities.

In February 2021, Yolanda will release her first book, Let's Chat About Love: Romantic Love, Self-Love and the Ultimate, God's Love. She is also working on her own TV show slated to hit a streaming network in 2021.

Fun facts: Yolanda is called by her friends and even business peers as "Boss Lady", "Quiet Storm" and "Mentor" because of her natural gift of leadership, her quiet yet powerful demeanor, and her spirit to motivate and inspire. She has two adult children, and three grandchildren. Her daughter is alum of Howard University and is a teacher, author, and entrepreneur. Her son is a grad student at Mount Saint Mary's University, Los Angeles majoring in Film Production and Media Communication.

The Birth to My Purpose
The Journey to Motherhood

She speaks, she writes, she leads, she initiates, she motivates, and she inspires!

The Birth to My Purpose
The Journey to Motherhood

Unplanned... But Purpose Was Birthed

"I cannot thank God enough for the journey and honor or the craziness that ensues on this path to motherhood".

The title of becoming a "Mother" sounds like a merit badge, almost a recognition for lifetime achievement, and yes, it is that, in my opinion. We hear words like Motherland, Mother Earth, Mother Nature, and above all, Mother Goddess encompassing everything from conception to safety and sustenance. These words reflect the powers, rights, privileges, and duties connected with the nature of becoming a "mother." As child, I saw my mother, grandmothers, aunt-mothers as compassionate, nurturing, sensitive, and efficient people who were constantly at work. It never even crossed my mind that there was a journey to them becoming a mom.

Yes, I wanted to be a mother, one day. Of course, I wanted the husband, the house, the dog, the white picket fence and two children. However, I was not the one that was all "goo goo gaga" over babies. I never babysit, never changed a diaper, never played with a baby. I just was not intrigued by all of that. So, never in my wildest dreams, I nor anyone that knew me would have predicted that my journey to motherhood would begin when it did.

I was beyond shocked and scared, yet I embraced the journey.

The Birth to My Purpose
The Journey to Motherhood

The journey to motherhood begins long before we have our baby in our arms, obviously; it begins when we conceive them in our womb. Yes! The wonder of life, the influence of mother nature strikes, and the realization sets in, right from the moment of conception, "I am not alone now. Something extraordinary, indeed a part of my flesh and blood, is inside me, rising at its rate, wholly dependent on me. From now on, I am never alone; two lives in one, I have a little life inside me."

I know, that sounds so beautiful, motherly, and wonderful. However, I left out the part about two teenagers (17 was the age) making the adult decision to have sex and finding themselves in a situation that they did not bet on They had created what would be a mini version of them, and a life of responsibilities. These were not even ready for a committed relationship, let alone something that would bond them together for life. That is my story in a nutshell.

My journey to motherhood began when I was just 17, as I just mentioned. Fortunately, I had graduated high school. Unfortunately, I had just started my freshman year of college. My best friend and I had moved into our very own apartment, well campus apartment. We were ready for an amazing first year college experience. An experience it was. I was literally pregnant from my first month to the last month of my first year. *Welp, there went my college life;* no fun, no parties, no hookups; although a hook was the last thing I needed.

Can you imagine being a black girl, amongst primarily non-black peers... attending class and walking

The Birth to My Purpose
The Journey to Motherhood

around pregnant at a major university? Now that I think about, it is probably why my daughter is so intelligent. As she was developing inside of me, I was learning on a higher level, I suppose.

I would have never imagined I would begin my journey to motherhood at such a young age; *pregnant at 17 and baby at 18.* I know some would say, at least you were not 14, 15 or 16. I still say, I was too young.

My aunt said, I was way to spoiled to be bringing a child in to the world at the age of 18.

That resonated in my head for a while, and abortion did cross my mind. Not sure if it was my belief in God or my denial of being pregnant that kept me away from a planned parenthood clinic. I know I mention that the father was also 17 at the time of conception, but did I mention it was also his first year of college but at another university, imagine that.

The journey was not so bad in the first few months, but once that baby bump started to show, it became very awkward. However, I did not let it stop me from attending classes. I laugh about those days now because I would have my snacks and lunch with me all-packed and often ate in class. I mean, a pregnant woman cannot wait until a three-hour class is over. Surprisedly, I was not frowned upon; at least, I did not notice any frowns, so that was cool. No one made me feel out of place. I was determined to stay in school, and I did.

The Birth to My Purpose
The Journey to Motherhood

One of the hardest things on my journey was telling my mom. She was disappointed but she had my older brother at 18, so she understood the struggle. It must have been a generational thing, but Glory to God, my daughter broke that cycle. A few days after telling my mom, she came to me and said, I would need to apply for financial assistance. Sheesh, I certainly did not want to do all that. Nonetheless, I swallowed my pride and did what I needed to do to ensure I had money, food, and health insurance to take care of my baby.

The nine-month journey went by fast. My pregnancy was good. I did have the nipple pain, frequent urination and I had moments of being extra sleepy but that was about it. I was in great shape. I went to all my appointments. I took my prenatal pills. I did everything Dr. Benjamin advised.

It was the morning of June 14, 1989, that the journey got intense. I was in labor!

My two friends, who were cousins to my unborn child, came over immediately. They had me walking around the block over and over. Supposedly that would make my labor and delivery easy, but it did not.

After 32 hours of labor, being delusional, extremely exhausted, seeing a worried mom and the tears of my friends, Dr. Benjamin finally says it is time to push. I pushed and pushed, and that little girl did not budge. We could see the head, but that was it. An emergency C-section became a must. All I remember is bright beaming lights

The Birth to My Purpose
The Journey to Motherhood

and the entire medical team moving at a very rapid place. It freaked me out! The last thing I remember saying before the anesthesia kicked it was, "Please, slow down".

The journey had just moved too fast, literally. I was terrified.

Not sure how long I was out, but I can recall the nurse saying, "Yolanda, wake up. You have a baby girl". WOW! The nurse showed me this little beautiful, yellow banana, as I described her that day. I could not believe; I was a mother. It was beautiful, yet overwhelming.

It was only a few hours after seeing her that I literally blacked out, literally.

I recall my mom walking into my room, and as she walked towards me, she was fading away. I blacked out, and when I woke up, I had no sight. I could not see; I could not see! I could hear in my mother's voice and my doctor's voice; they were freaked out as well. I lost my sight for 48 hours. I remember praying to God to please help me. When I woke up that morning (two days later) and could see the sun shining through my hospital window, I just thanked the *Most- High*, my God, my Savior, my All and All. I remember uttering the words, "Thank You, Jesus!" Now, I was ready to go home. My baby had already gone home. She was waiting for her mother.

It was never determined what caused the loss of sight. I summed it up as… my brain could not comprehend the destination of my journey; I just was not ready nor was I ready for the new journey I was about to embark on. My

The Birth to My Purpose
The Journey to Motherhood

journey to motherhood, did not seem to have been tough physically, but the mental aspect finally caught up with my physical. The journey was an undertaking. I handled, it but it was indeed a struggle.

The journey changed my entire life. It gave me a new perspective, and despite the detours along they journey, I did it again seven and half years later. This time I was mentally stronger and much more prepared. I had a natural birth; my second child, my son. At 26, I was a mother to a daughter and son… what a journey!

My children are my inspiration for everything that I do. The title—MOMMY—did not sound super sexy until I became one nor did I realize it was part of my purpose.

The Birth to My Purpose

The God Almighty created this whole universe, hung up a sky over our heads, adorned it with stars, rising and setting sun, making flowers bloom, and continuing life on Earth. Do you think, he did all that just so it is here?

No!

He had a purpose, just as He did when He created us.

If a leaf takes birth from just a sprout, grow, and then fall off to its final abode, aren't we humans, the best creation, ought to have a purpose in this life? Little did I know that the Journey to Motherhood would prepare me for the Birth of My Purpose. Yes, I was only 17 and no I was not married but thank God for his forgiveness, his mercy, and his grace.

The Birth to My Purpose
The Journey to Motherhood

Much like conceiving a child, one's purpose must be conceived. You must get intimate with God through prayer and studying the word.

Much like the birth of a child, the birth of a purpose can be uncomfortable. There is a process you must go through. You go through trimesters/stages and each stage brings a different mood, different craving, a different size.

By walking into your purpose, you undergo a whole thought process from uncertainty and denial to acceptance and realization. As humans, we tend to deny the things that do not register to our mind, to the point where it becomes hard to continue anymore; eventually, we tend to accept the reality.

When I found out I was pregnant, it took time for me to accept it. I had no idea that my journey would be preparing me for something greater than I could ever have imagined.

For anyone that tells you that you are not capable mentally, spiritually, and physically to give birth to purpose; it is time to shut it out and take control of your life. I went blind for 48 hours, but I stood on my faith, pushed through the blindness until I woke up and could see. At time, my purpose was my child and need to push through the fears.

If today you are here, reading this, know that you have purpose. Prepare your body, your mind and soul for conception and then delivery. Stay motivated! When I look back at that time, the only thing I remember is how

The Birth to My Purpose
The Journey to Motherhood

everything that happened made me stronger and gave me a path to continue, for good, with all my heart. Our purpose is always bigger than we can imagine.

Once you are at ease, new ways open, you start seeing the possibilities that were nowhere near to be seen, and everything automatically starts aligning with you. Let nothing stop you from birthing your purpose. When you think that you can no longer do anything, that you have hit rock bottom and you feel overwhelmed by life, that is the moment for you to strive even harder and remain focused for you to give birth to your purpose.

Hard times test us and shape our character to birth our true purpose.

OH, I did finish college. No white picket fence but I did get that house and I eventually got married to my son's father, although I am now divorced. Fortunately, my now "adult children" do have great relationships with their dads. They are two amazing young adults who inspire me! All things really do work together for good for those who have faith and believe. I am now an empty nester, but I finally got that dog. It has not been that long since, I gave Birth to My Purpose, but I am living it to the fullest and thriving in it! To God be the Glory!

The Birth to My Purpose
The Journey to Motherhood

Chapter Six

Purpose Birthed Through Pain

Alexis Chavers

The Birth to My Purpose
The Journey to Motherhood

Alexis Chavers, I am a proud mother of six wonderful angels, affectionately known as "The Crew". I am also the Owner of Diamond Touch Cleaning & Lawn Services and a Family Engagement Specialist for Illinois Action for Children. Packed with passion and full of compassion, I use my platform as a Family Engagement Specialist to boldly advocate for at risk families while assisting them in identifying barriers, and developing action plans to reach their goals. As an owner of a small business my heart thrives off being able to provide jobs, specifically for young mothers. As a pillar in my church, I serve on the leadership team where I minister on the worship team and through dance. God also uses me to minister to young ladies of the church through our discipleship ministry, "Girls of Glory". I aspire to make a positive impact in the lives of young women throughout Chicago as God continues to direct her path.

The Birth to My Purpose
The Journey to Motherhood

Purpose Birthed Through Pain

Second year college student, praise dancer, part time employee and a responsible daughter. I was a young lady whose goals were contradictory to everything around her. That was 19-year-old me! Smashing goals, breaking generational curses and making my momma proud. I'm sure wherever my Dad was, he was proud too but that's a story for another book. This year of my life was filled with highs, lows and everything in between. I'm an avid believer that our journeys are not for everyone to understand, however, our stories of how we became, overcame and fought through is not only a testament of God's glory but an instrument of motivation and inspiration for the next woman. A Journey, by definition, is "the act of traveling from one place to another." New places require us to leave our comfort zone, introduces us to sights we haven't seen before and meet people we otherwise wouldn't have cross paths with. As a byproduct our perspectives are shifted, we speak differently, we walk differently, our tolerance level changes, change is inevitable. Follow me as I take you on a snippet of my journey through motherhood.

June 2003 my monthly visitor was missing in action, immediately the first thing that came to mind was "I'm pregnant". A positive store-bought pregnancy test confirmed. After gathering the courage to tell my mom, she dismissed the pregnancy stick which displayed the positive

The Birth to My Purpose
The Journey to Motherhood

result and told me it was defective. I stood confidently to inform her that I had bought the most expensive test on the shelf, so it had to be accurate. I was 19 years old, lol. But see this minor detail is important, because at the moment I felt that I was carrying a child, I immediately wanted "the best" for it. in my 19-year-old mind purchasing the best rated pregnancy test kit was choosing the best for my child. Later that evening my mom suggested that maybe I was stressed. Who me? Couldn't be.

Mom scheduled a Dr's appointment, which also confirmed that I was indeed carrying a baby. I saw the pain and disappointment in my mother eyes, as she told me that I would have to get an abortion. It stung my heart to know I've caused the hurt that she was feeling. Though she may have been speaking out of those emotions, my maternal state went into full drive protective mode. No one was going to force me to abort my child!

A thick cloud of tension lingered in our home for a few weeks. I received phone calls from family and church family with less-than-ideal comments, opinions and statements. "How could you make such poor decision"? "So much potential and you're throwing it away". "Do you really think the father will stay?" And the worse comment of them all, "This is selfish of you. Do you see what you're doing to your mom? This will be her baby, not yours." In that moment every move that I made was for the future of my baby. Every negative word and doubtful statement had now become the very bricks I used to build a solid foundation for our future. I decided to name my unborn

The Birth to My Purpose
The Journey to Motherhood

child "Jireh", which means "the Lord will provide". I knew without a shadow of a doubt that God would carry us through and provide for us.

A mother's love is all-embracing, all-accepting, a safe place and a place of support. It's forgiving and apologetic and fills a place that no other love can. After my mom's initial reaction subsided, she begins operating once more in the very love that I described. Morning sickness was kicking my butt in my first trimester! I'd vomit and cry out for my mom and she'll be right there. Every other prenatal appointment she was there. Every night I'll feel her touch my head and my belly, praying blessings over me and my baby. The highlight of some of our days was watching my very active fetus do somersaults in my belly. As big as I was getting it didn't stop me from curling up next to my mom like I was a baby. I knew I would be a good mom because I had a great mom.

Monday December 1st, 2003, I'm in my third trimester, I woke up excited to attend my prenatal appointment that afternoon after class. Though you feel your baby moving inside of you, it's so exciting hearing your child's heart beat through the doppler device. Before leaving out for class, my mom asked if I wanted her to meet me at my prenatal appointment. I had already planned for my child's father to meet me there and I would spend a few nights with him. Ultimately, I decided I would spend the night out over the weekend instead. After leaving the prenatal appointment, we hung out a little bit, but was conscious of the time, because some of the best black

The Birth to My Purpose
The Journey to Motherhood

comedy shows were scheduled for Monday night's beginning at 7pm.

Settling in that evening, warming up plates of the last of Thanksgiving leftovers, my sister and I sat on the couch waiting for our mom to join us in the living room. After my mom grabbed her Sierra Mist out of the freezer, she walked over to sit on the floor next to the couch. As she sat down, I heard her say "Somebody help me". That was the last thing I heard her say. As I was going along this journey to motherhood, preparing for the most exciting time of my life, I suddenly and unexpectedly lost someone I've loved my entire life. How was I to become a mom when I no longer had one?

If I'm honest, for a moment, I wasn't sure if I wanted to be a mom anymore. I was torn, broken, hurt and angry with God! Uncertainty, fear, confusion and doubt had begun to take root in my mind and bitterness in my heart. Not only was I a first-time mom, but I had to become a "Mom" to my 12-year-old sister. Neither of our fathers were around. It was just us. I had no clue what to do or where I was going.

February 1st, I went into labor. I remember as I laid on the table and the Dr's instructed me to push, I stopped after a few pushes. With tears in my eyes, I said I can't do it! I was weak from the constant mourning; it undoubtedly took a toll on my mental and physical body. I remember thinking it would be best if this baby doesn't enter the world, I have nothing to give. How could I raise a baby

The Birth to My Purpose
The Journey to Motherhood

when all my heart felt was agony? I wanted to die. The pain was unbearable, and I am not talking about childbirth.

My aunt stood to the left of my bedside holding my hand and with the most calming voice coached me through. When I looked at her, there was a transfer of strength from her to me. Towards the foot of the bed, I looked at my sister, and knew I was all she had. To the right of my bed was my mom's picture and as the tears rolled down my cheeks, I decided that I would be a good mom, because I had a great mom. With renewed strength, I pushed and I pushed, confidently knowing that God had already equipped me with everything I needed to be the mother, sister and woman he had called me to be.

My baby girl was born on Monday, February 2, 2004 at 2:18am. The most beautiful baby I have ever laid eyes on. As she looked at me, I knew I needed her just as much as she needed me. I had an abundance of love left to give, specially reserved for her. Innate abilities, much like super powers begin to emerge after her birth. Deciphering her distressed cries, from her hungry cries or sleepy cries became an amazing ability I never thought I would need. The production of milk my body produced to feed my child on demand was mind blowing!

This journey to motherhood taught me that no matter what we face as women, regardless of the pain our heart endures, there is always room to love the child we created. This journey showed me how my strength was developed out of my weakness. Not only had my body changed, but my mind as well. This journey requires you

The Birth to My Purpose
The Journey to Motherhood

to evolve, at least for me it did. Elevation was a must. Staying focus on my goals was non-negotiable. Being flexible to accommodate my children needs was and still is necessary. Through my pain my purpose was birthed. God has given me a heart for young mothers. A passion to guide those who were left without a mom to walk with them along their journey.

Six kids later I am still walking through this journey. Who knew that a heart could hold so much love? Psalm 127: 3 -5 says, "Children are a heritage from the Lord. The fruit of the womb is a reward, like arrows in the hand of a warrior, so are the children of one's youth. How blessed is the man whose quiver is filled with them; they shall not be ashamed, but they shall speak with the enemies in the gate." I don't take these gifts for granted. My greatest blessings are the children I've be chosen to birth and care for. For me each birth was like the first time. The anticipation never lessens. As every pregnancy is different so is each child. I love the excitement that comes with learning the different personalities of the miniature versions of yourself and the person you love.

Motherhood comes with an advanced degree in life. It requires us to sharpen up or develop a vast number of skills that will carry us throughout this journey, learning some right away and others when we get to the seasons that force us to obtain it. In motherhood we have to wear a multitude of hats and most often more than one at a time. We run households, schedule play dates, book sports and extracurricular activities, plan trips and make lunches. We

The Birth to My Purpose
The Journey to Motherhood

are drivers, bouncers', doctors, travel agents, chefs, receptionists and ministers all rolled into one. I have learned on this journey, because of all the hats we wear, and the many roles we play, that it is ok for "superwoman" to hang up her cape sometimes. Self-care is essential! We cannot pour from an empty cup.

When I look back at the person, I was the summer of 2002, I barely even recognize that young lady. Not that I've lost myself, but it's just that I've grown and developed so much more rapidly in the years I've spent in the best "hood"! My children are my greatest investment and the return on that investment is unmatchable! My greatest hope is to someday walk with my daughter as she enters into motherhood, to guide her, support her and continue to love her through it. Every day I pray to God that my mom is proud of the mother I am and the woman she has helped me become. I am ever so grateful for the 20 years I was able to spend with her, learning how to love and placing God in the center of all things. Though I would have loved to have had a hundred and one more year with my mom, she truly did prepare me for life and motherhood through her actions, her teachings, prayers and her modeling. Motherhood is the greatest gift God gave me and the greatest gift my mom gave me was God. If I don't know anything else, I know that I can do all things through Christ who strengthens me!

The Birth to My Purpose
The Journey to Motherhood

The Birth to My Purpose
The Journey to Motherhood

Conclusion

Thank you for taking the time to read "*The Birth to My Purpose, The Journey to Motherhood*"

In this anthology, we the Authors, wanted to share our story of our journey to motherhood to be able to help you in whatever journey stage that you may be in. Remember you can and will get through this.

The bible says in Isaiah 40:31 "But they who wait for the Lord shall renew their strength; they shall mount up with wings like eagles; they shall run and not be weary; they shall walk and not faint." I ask that you hold on, hold on to your faith, do not faint, your parenting is not in vain.

Remember that your prayers are being heard. You have to continue to love on you, continue to love on your children, continue to heal the pains and grow into the best parent that you know how to be, continue to have faith in knowing that God is working on your behalf. It will all work out in due time, in due season, and all in God's timing….

Thank you!

Invisible Daughter LLC
Under the umbrella of Mikkita Moore LLC
www.mikkitamoore.com

The Birth to My Purpose
The Journey to Motherhood